RENAMED
AND
REDEEMED

Operating In The Name Of Jesus

SYLLABUS

World Harvest Church · Columbus, Ohio

All scripture references have been
taken from the King James Version of
the Bible, unless otherwise indicated.

ISBN No. 1-880244-02-0

Published by:

P.O. Box 32932
Columbus, Ohio 43232

PREFACE

Exodus 20:7 Thou shalt not take the name of the LORD thy God in vain; for the LORD will not hold him guiltless that taketh his name in vain. (KJV)

We usually understand this scripture to mean that we are forbidden to use God's name in any profane context. There is, however, a profanity more obscene than any other that we oftentimes overlook. That profanity is taking the name "Christian" but failing to walk in the power of that name.

Most married men received a graphic illustration of this principle when they found out that their wife had not taken their name in vain. No, she took it to the bank, to department stores and other places that accept checks and credit cards. She took her husband's name, and all he had became hers to share.

God would have us learn this lesson. When we take the name of Jesus, we become "joint heirs" with him, and all that belongs to the Father becomes available to us.

I trust this syllabus will enable you to come to understand what it means to be renamed and redeemed.

SYLLABUS

RENAMED AND REDEEMED
Operating In The Name Of Jesus

INDEX

RELINQUISHED HERITAGE

When Adam chose to eat of the tree of the knowledge of good and evil, he got just what he asked for -- the knowledge of every evil disease and atrocity and the awareness of every good and perfect gift, which lay just beyond his sin-infected reach.

I inherited sin, sorrow and sickness, and a home in hell. The awfulness of sin is this: In my name, I inherited sin and death. My blood line is contaminated. The Adamic nature is present at birth, and it works its deadly work until at the age of accountability -- (that time when a person is aware of right and wrong and chooses wrong; it varies from individual to individual) -- it comes into full dominance.

Paul in Romans 7:24 expresses the heart cry of all humanity:
O unhappy and pitiable and wretched man that I am! who will release and deliver me from (the shackles of) this body of death? (AMP)

1. **GOD WILL NOT JUSTIFY SIN.** GOD IS OBLIGATED TO OBEY HIS OWN LAWS. HIS PERFECT SENSE OF JUSTICE DEMANDS A PRICE PAID FOR SIN. THE PRICE IS BEYOND MAN'S ABILITY TO PAY. ADAM SURRENDERED ONE SINLESS LIFE, AND THE ONLY ACCEPTABLE PRICE WOULD BE ONE SINLESS LIFE.

   Exodus 23:7 *Keep thee far from a false matter; and the innocent and righteous slay thou not: for I will not justify the wicked.*

2. **THERE IS NO PARTIALITY WITH GOD.** YOUR PERSONALITY, GIFTINGS OR ATTRIBUTES MAKE NO DIFFERENCE AT ALL. GOD'S ABHORRENCE OF SIN IS THE SAME, REGARDLESS OF WHO COMMITS IT.

   Psalms 5:5 *The foolish shall not stand in thy sight: thou hatest all workers of iniquity.*

3. **GOD IS CONSISTENT IN HIS HATRED OF SIN.** THERE IS NO SHADOW OF TURNING WITH GOD. HE IS ALWAYS IN THE ETERNAL NOW. HE IS THE SAME YESTERDAY, TODAY AND FOREVER. MANY TIMES, AS PARENTS, WE ALLOW OUR MOOD OR FEELINGS TO CLOUD OUR DEALINGS WITH OUR CHILDRENS' SHORTCOMINGS. NOT SO WITH GOD. IN A REAL SENSE, HIS CONSISTENCY IS A COMFORT. WE ALWAYS KNOW WHERE WE STAND WITH HIM.

> Psalms 7:11 *God judgeth the righteous, and God is angry with the wicked every day.*

4. **EVEN THE REMEMBRANCE OF THE WICKED SHALL PERISH.** GOD CANNOT COUNTENANCE SIN. THERE ARE ONLY TWO WAYS SIN CAN BE COVERED: (1) BY HELL. ONE OF THE DEFINITIONS OF THE HEBREW WORD FOR HELL IS "A COVERED PLACE"; (2) BY THE BLOOD. THE JEWISH CELEBRATION OF THE DAY OF ATONEMENT IS YOM KIPPUR. THE WORD KIPPUR MEANS A COVERING. WE GET OUR ENGLISH WORD CAP FROM IT. WHEN THE BLOOD WAS PLACED ON THE JUDGMENT SEAT ON THE ARK OF THE COVENANT, THE JUDGMENT SEAT BECAME THE MERCY SEAT.

> Psalms 9:5 *Thou hast rebuked the heathen, thou hast destroyed the wicked, thou hast put out their name for ever and ever.*

5. **IT ALL BEGAN IN THE GARDEN OF EDEN.**

> Gen 2:17 *But of the tree of the knowledge of good and evil, thou shalt not eat of it: for in the day that thou eatest thereof thou shalt surely die.*

6. **THE CURSE IS THE RESULT OF SIN.** BLESSING IS FLOWING IN THE PLAN OF GOD. CURSING IS FIGHTING THIS DIVINE FLOW. THERE ARE ONLY TWO WAYS TO SLIDE DOWN THE BANISTER OF LIFE: WITH THE GRAIN AND AGAINST THE GRAIN. AGAINST THE GRAIN, YOU GET SPLINTERS.

> Gen 3:16-19 *Unto the woman he said, I will greatly multiply thy sorrow and thy conception; in sorrow thou shalt bring forth children; and thy desire shall be to thy husband, and he shall rule over thee.*
>
> v. 17 *And unto Adam he said, Because thou hast hearkened unto the voice of thy wife, and hast eaten of the tree, of which I commanded thee, saying, Thou shalt not eat of it: cursed is the ground for thy sake; in sorrow shalt thou eat of it all the days of thy life;*
>
> v. 18 *Thorns also and thistles shall it bring forth to thee; and thou shalt eat the herb of the field;*
>
> v. 19 *In the sweat of thy face shalt thou eat bread, till thou return unto the ground; for out of it wast thou taken: for dust thou art, and unto dust shalt thou return.*

7. **GOD'S PATIENCE HAS A LIMIT.** THERE IS AN ACCEPTED TIME. TODAY, RIGHT NOW, IS ALL YOU ARE PROMISED. GOD IS A NOW GOD, AND SALVATION IS A NOW PROPOSITION.

> Gen 6:3 *And the LORD said, My spirit shall not always strive with man, for that he also is flesh: yet his days shall be an hundred and twenty years.*

8. **THE FLOOD WAS THE ANSWER TO SIN IN NOAH'S GENERATION.** GOD ALWAYS HAS AN ANSWER TO HIS PROBLEM. WHAT ANSWER DOES HE HAVE FOR YOU?

> Gen 6:7 *And the LORD said, I will destroy man whom I have created from the face of the earth; both man, and beast, and the creeping thing, and the fowls of the air; for it repenteth me that I have made them.*

> Gen 6:12-13 *And God looked upon the earth, and, behold, it was corrupt; for all flesh had corrupted his way upon the earth.*
>
> v. 13 *And God said unto Noah, The end of all flesh is come before me; for the earth is filled with violence through them; and, behold, I will destroy them with the earth.*

9. **THERE IS A WAY OUT.** THE WAY OUT IS THROUGH JESUS AND FAITH IN HIS HAME. HEBREWS 11:4 SAYS "BY FAITH ABEL OFFERED UNTO GOD A MORE EXCELLENT SACRIFICE THAN CAIN." ACCORDING TO GOD'S WORD, FAITH COMETH BY HEARING GOD'S WORD. WE HAVE ALWAYS ASSUMED THAT ABEL "LUCKED OUT" IN PLEASING GOD WITH HIS SACRIFICE, BUT EVIDENTLY GOD HAD SOMETHING TO SAY ON THE SUBJECT OF SACRIFICE. ABEL LISTENED; CAIN DIDN'T. YOUR WAY OUT DEPENDS ON HEARING AND OBEYING GOD'S WORD.

> Gen 4:7 *If thou doest well, shalt thou not be accepted? and if thou doest not well, sin lieth at the door. And unto thee shall be his desire, and thou shalt rule over him.*

RENUNCIATION OF NAME

1. **I ADMIT THE BANKRUPTCY OF MY NAME.** I RENOUNCE IT AS USELESS.

   When I do this, I LOSE MY POVERTY.

   The singing group "Frankie Valli & the Four Seasons" had a hit single in the '60's entitled, "Rag Doll". The song is a story of a well-to-do boy in love with a very poor girl. The hero says, such a pretty face should be dresed in lace. I can't understand what he sees in me, but behind the soot and rags, he sees a Cinderella that he wants. While we were yet sinners, Christ died for us.

2. **PROSPERITY IS A LIFE-TIME PROPOSITION.** WITH LONG LIFE GOD HAS PROMISED TO SATISFY US. SOMEONE HAS SAID: CHOOSE FAITH THAT HAS HAPPY OLD PEOPLE.

   > Gen 24:1 *And Abraham was old, and well stricken in age: and the LORD had blessed Abraham in all things.*

3. **PROSPERITY IS A FAMILY AFFAIR.** YOUR DECISION WILL AFFECT MORE THAN JUST YOU. THE WORD OF GOD STATES THAT SIN WILL BE VISITED UPON MANY GENERATIONS. THE OTHER SIDE OF THAT COIN IS EQUALLY TRUE. OBEDIENCE AND RIGHTEOUSNESS HAVE AN EQUALLY LONG REACH.

   > Gen 25:21 *And Isaac intreated the LORD for his wife, because she was barren: and the LORD was intreated of him, and Rebekah his wife conceived.*

4. **IF WE STAY IN THE FAMILY, WE WILL PROSPER.** EPHESIANS 6:13-14 SAYS: HAVING DONE ALL TO STAND, STAND. IT WOULD NOT MAKE SENSE TO DO ALL TO STAND AND THEN SIT.

Prov 28:19 *He that tilleth his land shall have plenty of bread: but he that followeth after vain persons shall have poverty enough.*

5. **I MUST OBEY TO PROSPER.** GOD'S LAWS WORK, BUT WE MUST OBEY THEM FOR THEM TO WORK FOR US.

Deut 29:9 *Keep therefore the words of this covenant, and do them, that ye may prosper in all that ye do.*

Joshua 1:7 *Only be thou strong and very courageous, that thou mayest observe to do according to all the law, which Moses my servant commanded thee: turn not from it to the right hand or to the left, that thou mayest prosper whithersoever thou goest.*

1 King 2:3 *And keep the charge of the LORD thy God, to walk in his ways, to keep his statutes, and his commandments, and his judgments, and his testimonies, as it is written in the law of Moses, that thou mayest prosper in all that thou doest, and whithersoever thou turnest thyself:*

1 Chr 22:13 *Then shalt thou prosper, if thou takest heed to fulfil the statutes and judgments which the LORD charged Moses with concerning Israel: be strong, and of good courage; dread not, nor be dismayed.*

6. **OPERATING IN HIS NAME IS FRUITFUL.** THE ONLY WAY TO SUCCESS IS TO UNDERSTAND THAT OUR SOURCE IS GOD.

Exodus 23:26 *There shall nothing cast their young, nor be barren, in thy land: the number of thy days I will fulfil.*

7. **TAKING HIS NAME, I MAKE FULL USE OF HIS REDEMPTION.**

> Lev 25:25 *If thy brother be waxen poor, and hath sold away some of his possession, and if any of his kin come to redeem it, then shall he redeem that which his brother sold.*

RENAMED AND REDEEMED

"Redeemed - how I love to proclaim it!   Redeemed by the blood of the Lamb. Redeemed through his infinite mercy, His child and forever I am." (Fanny J. Crosby)

> Romans 8:1 *There is therefore now no condemnation to them which are in Christ Jesus, who walk not after the flesh, but after the Spirit.*

The word "therefore" should always be checked to see what it's there for. In this scripture, therefore refers to chapters 3, 6 and 7. The meaning of the scripture is: As a result of our justification (chapter 3), because of our union with Christ (chapter 6), and because of our complete identification with Him (chapter 7), in light of these compelling truths, there is no (not one bit of) doom or condemnation to those who are in (union with) Christ Jesus (the anointed Savior).

The word translated "no" in this scripture is an emphatic form, and is even more emphatic, since in the Greek it is at the beginning of the sentence.

1. **TAKING GOD'S NAME CORRECTLY ERASES GUILT.** IN THE FOLLOWING SCRIPTURE, THE WORD "VAIN" MEANS TO USE IN A FALSE OR USELESS WAY.

   > Deut 5:11 *Thou shalt not take the name of the LORD thy God in vain: for the LORD will not hold him guiltless that taketh his name in vain.*

2. **IN HIS NAME, THERE IS NO CONDEMNATION.** THE HOLY GHOST INTRODUCES YOU TO THE FATHER. HE IS OUR RECOMMENDATION, OUR REFERENCE. HE BECOMES OUR CREDIT RATING.

Romans 8:1-2 *There is therefore now no condemnation to them which are in Christ Jesus, who walk not after the flesh, but after the Spirit.*

v. 2. *For the law of the Spirit of life in Christ Jesus hath made me free from the law of sin and death.*

1 John 1:7 *But if we walk in the light, as he is in the light, we have fellowship one with another, and the blood of Jesus Christ his Son cleanseth us from all sin.*

v. 8 *If we say that we have no sin, we deceive ourselves, and the truth is not in us.*

v. 9 *If we confess our sins, he is faithful and just to forgive us our sins, and to cleanse us from all unrighteousness.*

3 **THE ROAD TO RIGHTEOUSNESS IS THROUGH SONSHIP.** SONSHIP MEANS TO BE AN HEIR TO THE HEAVENLY FATHER. LET THE HOLY GHOST INTRODUCE YOU TO JEHOVAH TSIDKENU, THE LORD YOUR RIGHTEOUSNESS.

Romans 3:22 *Even the righteousness of God which is by faith of Jesus Christ unto all and upon all them that believe: for there is no difference:*

Romans 4:16 *Therefore it is of faith, that it might be by grace; to the end the promise might be sure to all the seed; not to that only which is of the law, but to that also which is of the faith of Abraham; who is the father of us all,*

Romans 5:2 *By whom also we have access by faith into this grace wherein we stand, and rejoice in hope of the glory of God.*

Romans 5:15-16 *But not as the offence, so also is the free gift. For if through the offence of one many be dead, much more the grace of God, and the gift by grace, which is by one man, Jesus Christ, hath abounded unto many.*

v. 16 *And not as it was by one that sinned, so is the gift: for the judgment was by one to condemnation, but the free gift is of many offences unto justification.*

A. **ADVANTAGES OF SONSHIP**

1 Cor 1:7-8 *So that ye come behind in no gift; waiting for the coming of our Lord Jesus Christ:*

v. 8 *Who shall also confirm you unto the end, that ye may be blameless in the day of our Lord Jesus Christ.*

1 Cor 15:10 *But by the grace of God I am what I am: and his grace which was bestowed upon me was not in vain; but I laboured more abundantly than they all: yet not I, but the grace of God which was with me.*

2 Cor 1:12 *For our rejoicing is this, the testimony of our conscience, that in simplicity and godly sincerity, not with fleshly wisdom, but by the grace of God, we have had our conversation in the world, and more abundantly to you-ward.*

B. **TRUE SONSHIP BRINGS BLESSING.**

1 Chr 22:11 *Now, my son, the LORD be with thee; and prosper thou, and build the house of the LORD thy God, as he hath said of thee.*

C. **OBEDIENCE IS THE MARK OF TRUE SONSHIP.** TO OBEY IS TO CARRY OUT ORDERS OR INSTRUCTIONS. TO BE FOUND FAITHFUL IN OBEDIENCE, WE MUST KNOW THE COMMANDS AND UNDERSTAND THE INSTRUCTIONS. A COMMON ADAGE IS: WHEN ALL ELSE FAILS, READ THE INSTRUCTIONS. ALL ELSE WILL FAIL, AND YOU WILL BE A FAILURE UNLESS YOU TURN TO GOD'S INSTRUCTIONS AND FOLLOW HIS WORD FOR YOUR LIFE.

Romans 5:19 *For as by one man's disobedience many were made sinners, so by the obedience of one shall many be made righteous.*

4. **TAKING HIS NAME ILLUSTRATES CHRIST IN ME.** MY HOPE OR EARNEST EXPECTATION OF GLORY IS THE FACT THAT CHRIST IS IN ME. CHRIST FOR ME IS A COMFORTING THOUGHT; CHRIST WITH ME IS AN EVER PRESENT HELP; BUT CHRIST IN ME IS MY HOPE OF GLORY.

Gal 1:15-16 *But when it pleased God, who separated me from my mother's womb, and called me by his grace,*

v. 16 *To reveal his Son in me, that I might preach him among the heathen; immediately I conferred not with flesh and blood:*

Eph 1:5-9 *Having predestinated us unto the adoption of children by Jesus Christ to himself, according to the good pleasure of his will,*

v. 6 *To the praise of the glory of his grace, wherein he hath made us accepted in the beloved.*

v. 7 *In whom we have redemption through his blood, the forgiveness of sins, according to the riches of his grace;*

v. 8 *Wherein he hath abounded toward us in all wisdom and prudence;*

v. 9 *Having made known unto us the mystery of his will, according to his good pleasure which he hath purposed in himself:*

Eph 1:1 *Paul, an apostle of Jesus Christ by the will of God, to the saints which are at Ephesus, and to the faithful in Christ Jesus:*

5. **WE TAKE HIS NAME BY FAITH.** EVERYTHING THAT WE APPROPRIATE FROM THE SPIRITUAL REALM IS OBTAINED THROUGH THE AGENCY OF FAITH. REMEMBER, WITHOUT FAITH, PLEASING GOD IS AN IMPOSSIBILITY.

Eph 2:8 *For by grace are ye saved through faith; and that not of yourselves: it is the gift of God:*

Eph 4:7 *But unto every one of us is given grace according to the measure of the gift of Christ.*

1 Thes 5:28 *The grace of our Lord Jesus Christ be with you. Amen.*

1 Tim 1:14 *And the grace of our Lord was exceeding abundant with faith and love which is in Christ Jesus.*

2 Tim 1:9 *Who hath saved us, and called us with an holy calling, not according to our works, but according to his own purpose and grace, which was given us in Christ Jesus before the world began,*

1 Pet 4:10 *As every man hath received the gift, even so minister the same one to another, as good stewards of the manifold grace of God.*

2 Pet 1:2 *Grace and peace be multiplied unto you through the knowledge of God, and of Jesus our Lord,*

6. **THERE IS "KEEPING" POWER IN HIS NAME.**

Jude 24 *Now unto him that is able to keep you from falling, and to present you faultless before the presence of his glory with exceeding joy,*

Acts 4:12 *Neither is there salvation in any other: for there is none other name under heaven given among men, whereby we must be saved.*

Acts 4:19 *But Peter and John answered and said unto them, Whether it be right in the sight of God to hearken unto you more than unto God, judge ye.*

Acts 2:21 *And it shall come to pass, that whosoever shall call on the name of the Lord shall be saved.*

Job 33:24 *Then he is gracious unto him, and saith, Deliver him from going down to the pit: I have found a ransom.*

Psalms 72:4 *He shall judge the poor of the people, he shall save the children of the needy, and shall break in pieces the oppressor.*

7. **DELIVERANCE COMES FROM TAKING HIS NAME.** IF YOU ARE BESET BY SATAN'S SNARES, YOU WASTE YOUR TIME IF YOU CALL ON ME. CALL ON HIM. BEFORE YOUR BRAIN CAN FORM HIS NAME, HE WILL SAY "I'M HERE."

Psalms 72:12-14 *For he shall deliver the needy when he crieth; the poor also, and him that hath no helper.*

v. 13 *He shall spare the poor and needy, and shall save the souls of the needy.*

v. 14 *He shall redeem their soul from deceit and violence: and precious shall their blood be in his sight.*

Isaiah 40:10-11 *Behold, the Lord GOD will come with strong hand, and his arm shall rule for him: behold, his reward is with him, and his work before him.*

v. 11 *He shall feed his flock like a shepherd: he shall gather the lambs with his arm, and carry them in his bosom, and shall gently lead those that are with young.*

Isaiah 43:25 *I, even I, am he that blotteth out thy transgressions for mine own sake, and will not remember thy sins.*

8. WHEN YOU TAKE THE NAME OF JESUS, YOU GAIN A HERITAGE.

A. I INHERIT ALL THAT HE INHERITS.

"I've got a mansion just over the hilltop in that bright land where we'll never grow old; and some day yonder, we will never more wander but walk on streets that are purest gold."

(Ira Stanphil)

B. HIS LAND BECOMES MY LAND.

Lev 20:24 *But I have said unto you, Ye shall inherit their land, and I will give it unto you to possess it, a land that floweth with milk and honey: I am the LORD your God, which have separated you from other people.*

Exodus 6:8 *And I will bring you in unto the land, concerning the which I did swear to give it to Abraham, to Isaac, and to Jacob; and I will give it you for an heritage: I am the LORD.*

C. **JESUS IS NOT SICK. I DON'T HAVE TO BE SICK.**

Deut 7:15 *And the LORD will take away from thee all sickness, and will put none of the evil diseases of Egypt, which thou knowest, upon thee; but will lay them upon all them that hate thee.*

D. **SATAN'S OPPOSITION HAS NO EFFECT ON JESUS.** IT SHOULD HAVE NONE ON ME. JESUS HAD AN EFFECTIVE COUNTER FOR EACH APPROACH OF SATAN. JESUS TOOK MAN'S PART IN RESISTING SATAN, FOR EXAMPLE, "MAN SHALL NOT LIVE BY BREAD ALONE." AS A MAN, JESUS DEFEATED SATAN, PROVING ONCE AND FOR ALL THAT WE CAN DEFEAT HIM TOO.

Exodus 1:12 *But the more they afflicted them, the more they multiplied and grew. And they were grieved because of the children of Israel.*

E. **AS CHILDREN OF THE HOUSE, WE ARE BROUGHT INTO HIS HERITAGE.** OUR DWELLING PLACE IS SUPPOSED TO BE THE SECRET PLACE OF THE MOST HIGH GOD. HE BROUGHT US OUT OF BONDAGE TO BRING US INTO HIS BLESSEDNESS.

Exodus 15:17 *Thou shalt bring them in, and plant them in the mountain of thine inheritance, in the place, O LORD, which thou hast made for thee to dwell in, in the Sanctuary, O Lord which thy hands have established.*

Exodus 23:25 *And ye shall serve the LORD your God, and he shall bless thy bread, and thy water; and I will take sickness away from the midst of thee.*

Psalms 2:7-8 *I will declare the decree: the LORD hath said unto me, Thou art my Son; this day have I begotten thee.*

v. 8 *Ask of me, and I shall give thee the heathen for thine inheritance, and the uttermost parts of the earth for thy possession.*

Psalms 5:11 *But let all those that put their trust in thee rejoice: let them ever shout for joy, because thou defendest them: let them also that love thy name be joyful in thee.*

Acts 20:32 *And now, brethren, I commend you to God, and to the word of his grace, which is able to build you up, and to give you an inheritance among all them which are sanctified.*

9. **WE BECOME LIKE OUR FATHER.** PARENTS NEVER TIRE OF SEEING THEMSELVES REPRODUCED IN THEIR CHILDREN. OUR HEAVENLY FATHER IS NO DIFFERENT. HE WANTS TO SEE HIS CHARACTERISTICS, I.E., LOVE, PEACE, AND JOY, IN US.

Heb 12:2 *Looking unto Jesus the author and finisher of our faith; who for the joy that was set before him endured the cross, despising the shame, and is set down at the right hand of the throne of God.*

10. **JUSTIFICATION**

Titus 3:7 *That being justified by his grace, we should be made heirs according to the hope of eternal life.*

10. **THE HOLY SPIRIT (THE COMFORTER) HAS BEEN SENT AS OUR COVENANT ATTORNEY TO ENSURE OUR INHERITANCE.** I DON'T KNOW WHO WROTE IT, BUT THERE IS A LITTLE CHORUS THAT SAYS: "HE SIGNED THE DEED IN HIS ATONING BLOOD. HE EVER LIVES TO MAKE HIS PROMISE SURE. WHEN ALL THE HOSTS OF HELL MARCH IN TO MAKE A SECOND CLAIM, THEY ALL MARCH OUT AT THE MENTION OF HIS NAME."

Psalms 5:11 *But let all those that put their trust in thee rejoice: let them ever shout for joy, because thou defendest them: let them also that love thy name be joyful in thee.*

Psalms 20:1 *The LORD hear thee in the day of trouble; the name of the God of Jacob defend thee;*

Psalms 59:1 *Deliver me from mine enemies, O my God: defend me from them that rise up against me.*

Romans 3:22 *Even the righteousness of God which is by faith of Jesus Christ unto all and upon all them that believe: for there is no difference:*

Romans 4:4 *Now to him that worketh is the reward not reckoned of grace, but of debt.*

Romans 5:15-16 *But not as the offence, so also is the free gift. For if through the offence of one many be dead, much more the grace of God, and the gift by grace, which is by one man, Jesus Christ, hath abounded unto many.*

v. 16 *And not as it was by one that sinned, so is the gift: for the judgment was by one to condemnation, but the free gift is of many offences unto justification.*

RIGHTEOUSNESS

1. **I MAY NOT FEEL LIKE IT OR LOOK LIKE IT, BUT I AM COUNTED RIGHTEOUS.**
A SHABBILY DRESSED MAN WALKED INTO A CLOTHING STORE. NONE OF THE
STORE PERSONNEL SEEMED TO WANT TO WAIT ON HIM, THAT WAS A VERY
SERIOUS MISTAKE. THE POORLY DRESSED MAN WAS ONE OF THE WEALTHIEST
MEN IN THAT CITY.

> Gen 15:6 *And he believed in the LORD; and he counted it to him for righteousness.*

> Lev 19:15 *Ye shall do no unrighteousness in judgment: thou shalt not respect the person of the poor, nor honour the person of the mighty: but in righteousness shalt thou judge thy neighbour.*

> Psalms 1:1-6 *Blessed is the man that walketh not in the counsel of the ungodly, nor standeth in the way of sinners, nor sitteth in the seat of the scornful.*

> v. 2 *But his delight is in the law of the LORD; and in his law doth he meditate day and night.*

> v. 3 *And he shall be like a tree planted by the rivers of water, that bringeth forth his fruit in his season; his leaf also shall not wither; and whatsoever he doeth shall prosper.*

> v. 4 *The ungodly are not so: but are like the chaff which the wind driveth away.*

1 Pet 3:12 For the eyes of the Lord are over the righteous, and his ears are open unto their prayers: but the face of the Lord is against them that do evil.

1 John 2:29 If ye know that he is righteous, ye know that every one that doeth righteousness is born of him.
Romans 10:4 For Christ is the end of the law for righteousness to every one that believeth.

C. MY CARNAL EFFORTS FRUSTRATE GOD'S GRACE, IT IS AN UNMERITED GIFT.

Gal 2:21 I do not frustrate the grace of God: for if righteousness come by the law, then Christ is dead in vain.

Gen 15:6 And he believed in the LORD; and he counted it to him for righteousness.

Psalms 143:11 Quicken me, O LORD, for thy name's sake: for thy righteousness' sake bring my soul out of trouble.

Romans 3:22 Even the righteousness of God which is by faith of Jesus Christ unto all and upon all them that believe: for there is no difference:

2. I COULD NOT PAY THE DEBT, SO HE PAID IT. "JESUS PAID IT ALL; ALL TO HIM I OWE."

Romans 4:4 Now to him that worketh is the reward not reckoned of grace, but of debt.

Romans 5:15-21 but not as the offence, so also is the free gift. For if through the offence of one many be dead, much more the grace of God, and the gift by grace, which is by one man, Jesus Christ, hath abounded unto many.

v. 16 *And not as it was by one that sinned, so is the gift: for the judgment was by one to condemnation, but the free gift is of many offences unto justification.*

v. 17 *For if by one man's offence death reigned by one; much more they which receive abundance of grace and of the gift of righteousness shall reign in life by one, Jesus Christ.)*

v. 18 *Therefore as by the offence of one judgment came upon all men to condemnation; even so by the righteousness of one the free gift came upon all men unto justification of life.*

v. 19 *For as by one man's disobedience many were made sinners, so by the obedience of one shall many be made righteous.*

v. 20 *Moreover the law entered, that the offence might abound. But where sin abounded, grace did much more bound:*

v. 21 *That as sin hath reigned unto death, even so might grace reign through righteousness unto eternal life by Jesus Christ our Lord.*

3. DELIVERANCE

A. GOD HAS PURPOSED TO HAVE A RIGHTEOUS REMNANT.

Gen 45:7 *And God sent me before you to preserve you a posterity in the earth, and to save your lives by a great deliverance.*

Psalms 3:3-4 *But thou, O LORD, art a shield for me; my glory, and the lifter up of mine head.*

v. 4 *I cried unto the LORD with my voice, and he heard me out of his holy hill. Selah.*

Psalms 4:3 *But know that the LORD hath set apart him that is godly for himself: the LORD will hear when I call unto him.*

Psalms 5:11 *But let all those that put their trust in thee rejoice: let them ever shout for joy, because thou defendest them: let them also that love thy name be joyful in thee.*

B. **GOD'S GREATEST BLESSING TO US IS DELIVERANCE.**

Psalms 5:12 *For thou, LORD, wilt bless the righteous; with favour wilt thou compass him as with a shield.*

Psalms 7:1 *O LORD my God, in thee do I put my trust: save me from all them that persecute me, and deliver me:*

Psalms 7:10 *My defence is of God, which saveth the upright in heart.*

Psalms 8:1 *O LORD our Lord, how excellent is thy name in all the earth! who hast set thy glory above the heavens.*

C. **FAITH IS STARING AT ADVERSE CIRCUMSTANCES AND PRAISING GOD. PRAISE BRINGS STRENGTH.**

Psalms 8:2 *Out of the mouth of babes and sucklings hast thou ordained strength because of thine enemies, that thou mightest still the enemy and the avenger.*

Psalms 9:9 *The LORD also will be a refuge for the oppressed, a refuge in times of trouble.*

1 John 4:4 *Ye are of God, little children, and have overcome them: because greater is he that is in you, than he that is in the world.*

1 John 5:18 *We know that whosoever is born of God sinneth not; but he that is begotten of God keepeth himself, and that wicked one toucheth him not.*

Col 2:14-15 *Blotting out the handwriting of ordinances that was against us, which was contrary to us, and took it out of the way, nailing it to his cross;*

v. 15 *And having spoiled principalities and powers, he made a shew of them openly, triumphing over them in it.*

D. **OUR WARFARE IS THE FIGHT OF FAITH.**

Eph 6:12 *For we wrestle not against flesh and blood, but against principalities, against powers, against the rulers of the darkness of this world, against spiritual wickedness in high places.*

Psalms 94:17 *Unless the LORD had been my help, my soul had almost dwelt in silence.*

Psalms 138:3 *In the day when I cried thou answeredst me, and strengthenedst me with strength in my soul.*

Psalms 143:11 *Quicken me, O LORD, for thy name's sake: for thy righteousness' sake bring my soul out of trouble.*

Daniel 9:18 *O my God, incline thine ear, and hear; open thine eyes, and behold our desolations, and the city which is called by thy name: for we do not present our supplications before thee for our righteousnesses, but for thy great mercies.*

E. **SATAN HAS A PLAN TO TAKE YOU OUT. GOD HAS A PLAN TO KEEP YOU IN.**

John 17:15 *I pray not that thou shouldest take them out of the world, but that thou shouldest keep them from the evil.*

Jude 24 *Now unto him that is able to keep you from falling, and to present you faultless before the presence of his glory with exceeding joy,*

Rev 3:10 *Because thou hast kept the word of my patience, I also will keep thee from the hour of temptation, which shall come upon all the world, to try them that dwell upon the earth.*

Mark 16:17 *And these signs shall follow them that believe; In my name shall they cast out devils; they shall speak with new tongues;*

Acts 16:18 *And this did she many days. But Paul, being grieved, turned and said to the spirit, I command thee in the name of Jesus Christ to come out of her. And he came out the same hour.*

Acts 5:16 *There came also a multitude out of the cities round about unto Jerusalem, bringing sick folks, and them which were vexed with unclean spirits: and they were healed every one.*

F. **GOD'S PLAN OF DELIVERANCE WILL SURPRISE SATAN AND US.**

Exodus 14:1-7 *And the LORD spake unto Moses, saying,*

v. 2 Speak unto the children of Israel, that they turn and encamp before Pihahiroth, between Migdol and the sea, over against Baalzephon: before it shall ye encamp by the sea.

v. 3 For Pharaoh will say of the children of Israel, They are entangled in the land, the wilderness hath shut them in.

v. 4 And I will harden Pharaoh's heart, that he shall follow after them; and I will be honoured upon Pharaoh, and upon all his host; that the Egyptians may know that I am the LORD. And they did so.

v. 5 And it was told the king of Egypt that the people fled: and the heart of Pharaoh and of his servants was turned against the people, and they said, Why have we done this, that we have let Israel go from serving us?

v. 6 And he made ready his chariot, and took his people with him:

v. 7 And he took six hundred chosen chariots, and all the chariots of Egypt, and captains over every one of them.

G. GOD WILL MAKE US BAIT IN THE TRAP.

Exodus 14:8-13 And the LORD hardened the heart of Pharaoh king of Egypt, and he pursued after the children of Israel: and the children of Israel went out with an high hand.

v. 9 But the Egyptians pursued after them, all the horses and chariots of Pharaoh, and his horsemen, and his army, and overtook them encamping by the sea, beside Pihahiroth, before

Baalzephon.

v. 10 *And when Pharaoh drew nigh, the children of Israel lifted up their eyes, and, behold, the Egyptians marched after them; and they were sore afraid: and the children of Israel cried out unto the LORD.*

v. 11 *And they said unto Moses, Because there were no graves in Egypt, hast thou taken us away to die in the wilderness? wherefore hast thou dealt thus with us, to carry us forth out of Egypt?*

v. 12 *Is not this the word that we did tell thee in Egypt, saying, Let us alone, that we may serve the Egyptians? For it had been better for us to serve the Egyptians, than that we should die in the wilderness.*

v. 13 *And Moses said unto the people, Fear ye not, stand still, and see the salvation of the LORD, which he will shew to you to day: for the Egyptians whom ye have seen to day, ye shall see them again no more for ever.*

H. **RELAX! GOD WILL FIGHT THE BATTLE.**

Exodus 14:14-16 *The LORD shall fight for you, and ye shall hold your peace.*

v. 15 *And the LORD said unto Moses, Wherefore criest thou unto me? speak unto the children of Israel, that they go forward:*

v. 16 *But lift thou up thy rod, and stretch out thine hand over the sea, and divide it: and the children of Israel shall go on dry ground through the midst of the sea.*

I. **WE ARE SAVED THROUGH HIS NAME.**

Psalms 54:1 *Save me, O God, by thy name, and judge me by thy strength.*

Job 33:24 *Then he is gracious unto him, and saith, Deliver him from going down to the pit: I have found a ransom.*

Psalms 72:4 *He shall judge the poor of the people, he shall save the children of the needy, and shall break in pieces the oppressor.*

Psalms 72:12-14 *For he shall deliver the needy when he crieth; the poor also, and him that hath no helper.*

v. 13 *He shall spare the poor and needy, and shall save the souls of the needy.*

v. 14 *He shall redeem their soul from deceit and violence: and precious shall their blood be in his sight.*

4. **QUICKENING LIFE**

When you see the word "quicken," substitute the word "life". It may not be good grammar, but it is true to the original text.

Psalms 80:18 *So will not we go back from thee: quicken us, and we will call upon thy name.*

Psalms 119:25 *My soul cleaveth unto the dust: quicken thou me according to thy word.*

Psalms 119:37 *Turn away mine eyes from beholding vanity;*

and quicken thou me in thy way.

Psalms 119:40 *Behold, I have longed after thy precepts: quicken me in thy righteousness.*

Psalms 119:50 *This is my comfort in my affliction: for thy word hath quickened me.*

A. **HE "LIFES" US BECAUSE HE LOVES US.**

Psalms 119:88 *Quicken me after thy lovingkindness; so shall I keep the testimony of thy mouth.*

Psalms 119:93 *I will never forget thy precepts: for with them thou hast quickened me.*

Psalms 119:107 *I am afflicted very much: quicken me, O LORD, according unto thy word.*

Psalms 119:149 *Hear my voice according unto thy lovingkindness: O LORD, quicken me according to thy judgment.*

Psalms 119:154 *Plead my cause, and deliver me: quicken me according to thy word.*

B. **HE "LIFES" US BECAUSE OF HIS MERCY.**

Psalms 119:156 *Great are thy tender mercies, O LORD: quicken me according to thy judgments.*

Psalms 119:159 *Consider how I love thy precepts: quicken me, O LORD, according to thy lovingkindness.*

Psalms 143:11 *Quicken me, O LORD, for thy name's sake: for thy righteousness' sake bring my soul out of trouble.*

Psalms 1:1 *Blessed is the man that walketh not in the counsel of the ungodly, nor standeth in the way of sinners, nor sitteth in the seat of the scornful.*

John 5:21 *For as the Father raiseth up the dead, and quickeneth them; even so the Son quickeneth whom he will.*

C. **HIS SPIRIT "LIFES" US.**

John 6:63 *It is the spirit that quickeneth; the flesh profiteth nothing: the words that I speak unto you, they are spirit, and they are life.*

Heb 5:9 *And being made perfect, he became the author of eternal salvation unto all them that obey him;*

Heb 6:17-19 *Wherein God, willing more abundantly to shew unto the heirs of promise the immutability of his counsel, confirmed it by an oath:*

v. 18 *That by two immutable things, in which it was impossible for God to lie, we might have a strong consolation, who have fled for refuge to lay hold upon the hope set before us:*

v. 19 *Which hope we have as an anchor of the soul, both sure and steadfast, and which entereth into that within the veil;*

D. **THE LIFE HE GIVES US IS ETERNAL. THE LIFE MY PARENTS GAVE ME IS TEMPORAL.**

1 John 2:25 *And this is the promise that he hath promised us, even eternal life.*

1 John 5:11-13 *And this is the record, that God hath given to us eternal life, and this life is in his Son.*

v. 12 *He that hath the Son hath life; and he that hath not the Son of God hath not life.*

v. 13 *These things have I written unto you that believe on the name of the Son of God; that ye may know that ye have eternal life, and that ye may believe on the name of the Son of God.*

1 John 5:20 *And we know that the Son of God is come, and hath given us an understanding, that we may know him that is true, and we are in him that is true, even in his Son Jesus Christ. This is the true God, and eternal life.*

Romans 4:17 *(As it is written, I have made thee a father of many nations,) before him whom he believed, even God, who quickeneth the dead, and calleth those things which be not as though they were.*

E. **THE SAME SPIRIT THAT GAVE JESUS LIFE GIVES ME LIFE.**

Romans 8:11 *But if the Spirit of him that raised up Jesus from the dead dwell in you, he that raised up Christ from the dead shall also quicken your mortal bodies by his Spirit that dwelleth in you.*

Job 10:12 *Thou hast granted me life and favour, and thy visitation hath preserved my spirit.*

Psalms 143:11 *Quicken me, O LORD, for thy name's sake: for thy righteousness' sake bring my soul out of trouble.*

Eph 3:16 *That he would grant you, according to the riches of his glory, to be strengthened with might by his Spirit in the inner man;*

Eph 6:10 *Finally, my brethren, be strong in the Lord, and in the power of his might.*

Titus 3:7 *That being justified by his grace, we should be made heirs according to the hope of eternal life.*

1 Pet 5:10 *But the God of all grace, who hath called us unto his eternal glory by Christ Jesus, after that ye have suffered a while, make you perfect, stablish, strengthen, settle you.*

RECOGNITION IS IDENTIFICATION

1. ...AS HE IS, SO ARE WE IN THIS WORLD.

> 1 John 4:17 *Herein is our love made perfect, that we may have boldness in the day of judgment: because as he is, so are we in this world.*

In the latter part of the 19th century, a young man with a brillant new concept of industry went to one of New York's most powerful and influential business tycoons. The business man, desiring to hear the young man's idea and at the same time conduct some business on the floor of the New York stock exchange, suggested that they talk on the floor of the exchange. For 30 minutes, the two walked over the crowded floor of the exchange. The older man, quite impressed with the brilliant mind of the younger man, placed his hand in a fatherly manner on the younger man's shoulder.

At the conclusion of their talk, the successful investment banker said to the young man "That's a great idea. Go do it." The young man, trying to hide his disappointment, said "I had thought you might finance this project." The banker said, "For 30 minutes, I have walked before some of the most powerful men in the world with my hand on your shoulder. I have identified with you. Any one of these men will finance your plan."

> Gen 1:27 *So God created man in his own image, in the image of God created he him; male and female created he them.*
>
> Eph 2:4-7 *But God, who is rich in mercy, for his great love wherewith he loved us,*
>
> v. 5 *even when we were dead in sins, hath quickened us together with Christ, (by grace ye are saved;)*

v. 6 *and hath raised us up together, and made us sit together in heavenly places in Christ Jesus:*

v. 7 *that in the ages to come he might shew the exceeding riches of his grace in his kindness toward us through Christ Jesus.*

Heb 2:17 *Wherefore in all things it behoved him to be made like unto his brethren, that he might be a merciful and faithful high priest in things pertaining to God, to make reconciliation for the sins of the people.*

Heb 11:6 *But without faith it is impossible to please him: for he that cometh to God must believe that he is, and that he is a rewarder of them that diligently seek him.*

Psalms 2:7 *I will declare the decree: the LORD hath said unto me, Thou art my Son; this day have I begotten thee.*

2. **THE REVERSE IS ALSO TRUE.** WHATEVER I HAVE DONE, IT IS AS THOUGH HE DID IT AND PAID THE PENALTY FOR IT. WHATEVER I HAVE RECEIVED (AS A RESULT OF SIN), IT IS AS THOUGH HE RECEIVED IT.

Isaiah 53:4 *Surely He has born our griefs, sickness, weakness and distress and carried our sorrows, pain of punishment. (AMP)*

3. **NOT ONLY DO I IDENTIFY WITH CHRIST, HE IDENTIFIES WITH ME.** HIS POWER HAS BECOME MY POWER.

Acts 3:6 *Then Peter said, Silver and gold have I none; but such as I have give I thee: In the name of Jesus Christ of Nazareth rise up and walk.*

Acts 4:29 *And now, Lord, behold their threatenings: and grant unto thy servants, that with all boldness they may speak thy word,*

John 17:6 *I have manifested thy name unto the men which thou gavest me out of the world: thine they were, and thou gavest them me; and they have kept thy word.*

REPLETION

1. **A PERSON IS KNOWN BY HIS NAME.** HE IS HIS NAME. WHEN I TAKE THE NAME OF JESUS, I HAVE HIS SUBSTANCE. I HAVE HIM, ALL THAT HE HAS.

> Acts 2:38 *Then Peter said unto them, Repent, and be baptized every one of you in the name of Jesus Christ for the remission of sins, and ye shall receive the gift of the Holy Ghost.*

> Eph 1:22 *And hath put all things under his feet, and gave him to be the head over all things to the church*

> Eph 1:23 *Which is his body, the fulness of him that filleth all in all.*

> Eph 1:23 *And is filled by him who fills all things everywhere with his presence (Twentieth Century New Testament)*

> Eph 1:23 *The completeness of him who everywhere fills the universe with himself (Wey)*

> Eph 1:23 *Filled by him who fills everything everywhere (Gspd)*

> Eph 1:23 *The completion of him who everywhere and in all things is complete (Knox)*

> Eph 1:23 *And in that body lives fully the one who fills the whole universe (Phi)*

> Eph 1:23 *The fullness of him who himself receives the entire fullness of God (NEB)*

The word fullness comes from the Greek word pleroma, which means repletion, completion, what fills and or what is filled -- satisfaction.

Jesus fills the universe, good and bad, so He has dominion over all things. He covers them and fills them, changing and isolating them, becoming a buffer zone to protect His body. Like white blood cells, He neutralizes the poison by surrounding it and insulating His body from its harmful effect. This is not to say that Christ is a party to evil, only that through His omniscience and omnipresence He fills everything everywhere with His presence. (Ephesians 1:23 TCNT)

2. **HE IS IN HIS NAME.** I AM CONFESSING THAT HE IS MINE AND THAT I AM HIS.

> Mark 16:17 *And these signs shall follow them that believe; In my name shall they cast out devils; they shall speak with new tongues;*
>
> Acts 3:6 *Then Peter said, Silver and gold have I none; but such as I have give I thee: In the name of Jesus Christ of Nazareth rise up and walk.*
>
> Acts 4:29 *And now, Lord, behold their threatenings: and grant unto thy servants, that with all boldness they may speak thy word,*
>
> 1 Pet 4:10 *As every man hath received the gift, even so minister the same one to another, as good stewards of the manifold grace of God.*

RESIGNATION

1. **WHEN I RESIGN MY NAME, I SUBMIT TO HIM.** THE POWER AND AUTHORITY OF THE FATHER, HENCE, OUR POWER AND AUTHORITY, HINGES UPON SUBMISSION TO JESUS.

> John 14:9 *Jesus saith unto him, Have I been so long time with you, and yet hast thou not known me, Philip? he that hath seen me hath seen the Father; and how sayest thou then, Show us the Father?*

> Luke 22:41-42 *And he was withdrawn from them about a stone's cast, and kneeled down, and prayed,*

> v. 42 *saying, Father, if thou be willing, remove this cup from me: nevertheless not my will, but thine, be done.*

> Luke 22:44 *And being in an agony he prayed more earnestly: and his sweat was as it were great drops of blood falling down to the ground.*

2. **WE SIN WHEN WE FAIL TO SUBMIT TO JESUS.**

> 2 John 8-9 *Look to yourselves, that we lose not those things which we have wrought, but that we receive a full reward.*

> v. 9 *Whosoever transgresseth, and abideth not in the doctrine of Christ, hath not God. He that abideth in the doctrine of Christ, he hath both the Father and the Son.*

Heb 5:7-9 *Who in the days of his flesh, when he had offered up prayers and supplications with strong crying and tears unto him that was able to save him from death, and was heard in that he feared;*

v. 8 *Though he were a Son, yet learned he obedience by the things which he suffered;*

v. 9 *And being made perfect, he became the author of eternal salvation unto all them that obey him;*

3. **SUBMISSION TO GOD ALWAYS WINS THE VICTORY.**

James 4:7 *Submit yourselves therefore to God. Resist the devil, and he will flee from you.*

Romans 13:1 *Let every soul be subject unto the higher powers. For there is no power but of God: the powers that be are ordained of God.*

James 4:4 *Ye adulterers and adulteresses, know ye not that the friendship of the world is enmity with God? whosoever therefore will be a friend of the world is the enemy of God.*

1 Cor 15:24 *Then cometh the end, when he shall have delivered up the kingdom to God, even the Father; when he shall have put down all rule and all authority and power.*

4. **GOD WORKS IN US TO MAKE HIS WILL OUR WILL.**

John 16:23 *And in that day ye shall ask me nothing. Verily, verily, I say unto you, Whatsoever ye shall ask the Father in my name, he will give it you.*

REPRESENTATION

Acts 4:29 *And now, Lord, behold their threatenings: and grant unto thy servants, that with all boldness they may speak thy word,*

Acts 26:22 *Having therefore obtained help of God, I continue unto this day, witnessing both to small and great, saying none other things than those which the prophets and Moses did say should come:*

1 Pet 4:10 *As every man hath received the gift, even so minister the same one to another, as good stewards of the manifold grace of God.*

1. **WHEN I TAKE HIS NAME, I AM PLEDGING TO DO ALL HE DID.** I ASSUME HIS POSTURE AND ATTITUDE TOWARD THE LOST AND DYING. THEREFORE:

    A. **WE WILL REPRESENT HIM IN PRAYER.**

    Matt 6:9-13 *After this manner therefore pray ye: Our Father which art in heaven, Hallowed be thy name.*

    v. 10 *Thy kingdom come. Thy will be done in earth, as it is in heaven.*

    v. 11 *Give us this day our daily bread.*

    v. 12 *And forgive us our debts, as we forgive our debtors.*

v. 13 *And lead us not into temptation, but deliver us from evil: For thine is the kingdom, and the power, and the glory, for ever. Amen.*

Luke 11:2-4 *And he said unto them, When ye pray, say, Our Father which art in heaven, Hallowed be thy name. Thy kingdom come. Thy will be done, as in heaven, so in earth.*

v. 3 *Give us day by day our daily bread.*

v. 4 *And forgive us our sins; for we also forgive every one that is indebted to us. And lead us not into temptation; but deliver us from evil.*

Luke 22:41-42 *And he was withdrawn from them about a stone's cast, and kneeled down, and prayed,*

v. 42 *saying, Father, if thou be willing, remove this cup from me: nevertheless not my will, but thine, be done.*

Luke 22:44 *And being in an agony he prayed more earnestly: and his sweat was as it were great drops of blood falling down to the ground.*

B. **WE KNOW, AS JESUS KNEW, THAT THE FATHER IS THE SOURCE.**

Heb 5:7 *Who in the days of his flesh, when he had offered up prayers and supplications with strong crying and tears unto him that was able to save him from death, and was heard in that he feared;*

1 Pet 3:12 *For the eyes of the Lord are over the righteous, and his ears are open unto their prayers: but the face of the Lord is against them that do evil.*

1 John 3:22-23 *And whatsoever we ask, we receive of him, because we keep his commandments, and do those things that are pleasing in his sight.*

v. 23 *And this is his commandment, That we should believe on the name of his Son Jesus Christ, and love one another, as he gave us commandment.*

Rev 5:8 *And when he had taken the book, the four beasts and four and twenty elders fell down before the Lamb, having every one of them harps, and golden vials full of odours, which are the prayers of saints.*

C. THROUGH FAITH IN PRAYER, WE DEFEAT SATAN.

Eph 6:12 *For we wrestle not against flesh and blood, but against principalities, against powers, against the rulers of the darkness of this world, against spiritual wickedness in high places.*

Acts 4:29 *And now, Lord, behold their threatenings: and grant unto thy servants, that with all boldness they may speak thy word,*

Phil 1:19 *For I know that this shall turn to my salvation through your prayer, and the supply of the Spirit of Jesus Christ,*

1 Pet 4:10 *As every man hath received the gift, even so minister the same one to another, as good stewards of the manifold grace of God.*

Mark 16:17 *And these signs shall follow them that believe; In my name shall they cast out devils; they shall speak with new tongues;*

2. WE REPRESENT HIM IN DRAWING OTHERS TO JESUS.

John 12:32 *And I, if I be lifted up from the earth, will draw all men unto me.*

Rev 22:7 *Behold, I come quickly: blessed is he that keepeth the sayings of the prophecy of this book.*

Acts 4:29 *And now, Lord, behold their threatenings: and grant unto thy servants, that with all boldness they may speak thy word,*

Acts 26:22 *Having therefore obtained help of God, I continue unto this day, witnessing both to small and great, saying none other things than those which the prophets and Moses did say should come:*

Gal 1:15-16 *But when it pleased God, who separated me from my mother's womb, and called me by his grace,*

v. 16 *To reveal his Son in me, that I might preach him among the heathen; immediately I conferred not with flesh and blood:*

1 Pet 4:10 *As every man hath received the gift, even so minister the same one to another, as good stewards of the manifold grace of God.*

Acts 1:8 *But ye shall receive power, after that the Holy Ghost is come upon you: and ye shall be witnesses unto me both in Jerusalem, and in all Judaea, and in Samaria, and unto the uttermost part of the earth.*

Acts 4:13 *Now when they saw the boldness of Peter and John, and perceived that they were unlearned and ignorant men, they marvelled; and they took knowledge of them, that they had been with Jesus.*

3. WE REPRESENT HIM THROUGH SUPERNATURAL WORKS.

Acts 4:14-33 *And beholding the man which was healed standing with them, they could say nothing against it.*

v. 15 *But when they had commanded them to go aside out of the council, they conferred among themselves,*

v. 16 *Saying, What shall we do to these men? for that indeed a notable miracle hath been done by them is manifest to all them that dwell in Jerusalem; and we cannot deny it.*

v. 17 *But that it spread no further among the people, let us straitly threaten them, that they speak henceforth to no man in this name.*

v. 18 *And they called them, and commanded them not to speak at all nor teach in the name of Jesus.*

v. 19 *But Peter and John answered and said unto them, Whether it be right in the sight of God to hearken unto you more than unto God, judge ye.*

v. 20 *For we cannot but speak the things which we have seen and heard.*

v. 21 *So when they had further threatened them, they let them go, finding nothing how they might punish them, because of the people: for all men glorified God for that which was done.*

v. 22 *For the man was above forty years old, on whom this miracle of healing was shewed.*

v. 23 *And being let go, they went to their own company, and reported all that the chief priests and elders had said unto them.*

v. 24 *And when they heard that, they lifted up their voice to God with one accord, and said, Lord, thou art God, which hast made heaven, and earth, and the sea, and all that in them is:*

v. 25 *Who by the mouth of thy servant David hast said, Why did the heathen rage, and the people imagine vain things?*

v. 26 *The kings of the earth stood up, and the rulers were gathered together against the Lord, and against his Christ.*

v. 27 *For of a truth against thy holy child Jesus, whom thou hast anointed, both Herod, and Pontius Pilate, with the Gentiles, and the people of Israel, were gathered together,*

v. 28 *For to do whatsoever thy hand and thy counsel determined before to be done.*

v. 29 *And now, Lord, behold their threatenings: and grant unto thy servants, that with all boldness they may speak thy word,*

v.30 *By stretching forth thine hand to heal; and that signs and wonders may be done by the name of thy holy child Jesus.*

v. 31 *And when they had prayed, the place was shaken where they were assembled together; and they were all filled with the Holy Ghost, and they spake the word of God with boldness.*

v. 32 *And the multitude of them that believed were of one heart and of one soul: neither said any of them that ought of the things which he possessed was his own; but they had all things common.*

v. 33 *And with great power gave the apostles witness of the resurrection of the Lord Jesus: and great grace was upon them all.*

4. WE REPRESENT HIM IN RESISTING THE DEVIL.

Matt 4:1-11 *Then was Jesus led up of the Spirit into the wilderness to be tempted of the devil.*

v. 2 *And when he had fasted forty days and forty nights, he was afterward an hungred.*

v. 3 *And when the tempter came to him, he said, If thou be the Son of God, command that these stones be made bread.*

v. 4 *But he answered and said, It is written, Man shall not live by bread alone, but by every word that proceedeth out of the mouth of God.*

v. 5 *Then the devil taketh him up into the holy city, and setteth him on a pinnacle of the temple,*

v. 6 *and saith unto him, If thou be the Son of God, cast thyself down: for it is written, He shall give his angels charge concerning thee: and in their hands they shall bear thee up, lest at any time thou dash thy foot against a stone.*

v. 7 *Jesus said unto him, It is written again, Thou shalt not tempt the Lord thy God.*

v. 8 *Again, the devil taketh him up into an exceeding high mountain, and sheweth him all the kingdoms of the world, and the glory of them;*

v. 9 *And saith unto him, All these things will I give thee, if thou wilt fall down and worship me.*

v. 10 *Then saith Jesus unto him, Get thee hence, Satan: for it is written, Thou shalt worship the Lord thy God, and him only shalt thou serve.*

v. 11 *Then the devil leaveth him, and, behold, angels came and ministered unto him.*

Mark 1:13 *And he was there in the wilderness forty days, tempted of Satan; and was with the wild beasts; and the angels ministered unto him.*

5. **WE TOO CAN COMMAND DEMONS IN JESUS' NAME.**

Acts 16:18 *And this did she many days. But Paul, being grieved, turned and said to the spirit, I command thee in the name of Jesus Christ to come out of her. And he came out the same hour.*

Heb 4:14-15 *Seeing then that we have a great high priest, that is passed into the heavens, Jesus the Son of God, let us hold fast our profession.*

V. 15 *For we have not an high priest which cannot be touched with the feeling of our infirmities; but was in all points tempted like as we are, yet without sin.*

James 4:7 *Submit yourselves therefore to God. Resist the devil, and he will flee from you.*

Acts 4:29 *And now, Lord, behold their threatenings: and grant unto thy servants, that with all boldness they may speak thy word,*

1 Cor 10:13 *There hath no temptation taken you but such as is common to man: but God is faithful, who will not suffer you to be tempted above that ye are able; but will with the temptation also make a way to escape, that ye may be able to bear it.*

RELIANCE

1. **IF I PRAY IN MY NAME, I CAN EXPECT ONLY WHAT I CAN DO.** PRAYING IN HIS NAME, I CAN RELY ON WHAT HE CAN DO. I MUST PRAY TO THE FATHER, IN THE NAME OF JESUS, THROUGH THE HOLY SPIRIT, ACCORDING TO THE WORD.

> Jer 33:3 *Call unto me, and I will answer thee, and shew thee great and mighty things, which thou knowest not.*

> Isaiah 43:26 *Put me in remembrance: let us plead together: declare thou, that thou mayest be justified.*

> Isaiah 55:11 *So shall my word be that goeth forth out of my mouth: it shall not return unto me void, but it shall accomplish that which I please, and it shall prosper in the thing whereto I sent it.*

> James 5:16 ...*The effectual fervent prayer of a righteous man availeth much. (KJV)*

> James 5:16 ...*The prayer of a righteous man is powerful and effective. (NIV)*

> James 5:16 ...*The earnest (heart-felt, continued) prayer of a righteous man makes tremendous power available -- dynamic in its working. (Amp.)*

2. GOD WILL GIVE YOU BOLDNESS TO ACT IN JESUS' NAME.

Acts 4:29 *And now, Lord, behold their threatenings: and grant unto thy servants, that with all boldness they may speak thy word,*

1 Pet 4:10 *As every man hath received the gift, even so minister the same one to another, as good stewards of the manifold grace of God.*

1 Pet 5:10 *But the God of all grace, who hath called us unto his eternal glory by Christ Jesus, after that ye have suffered a while, make you perfect, stablish, strengthen, settle you.*

Operating in the power of redemption, we can do all things through faith in His name. The redemptive names of God give us unique insight into His nature and His plan for us.

. . . .

"I AM"

Messiah
Deliverer, Anointed

Bread
Satisfier, Food

Light
Guide, Illuminator

Door
Way, Entrance

Shepherd
Keeper, Caregiver

Resurrection and Life
Life Giver, Death Destroyer

Vine
Sustainer

REDEMPTIVE NAMES OF THE LORD

1. The Redemptive Name,   YAHWEH, or Jehovah, I Am That I Am. Exodus 3:14-16

2. Jehovah Elohim   Genesis 2:4   The Lord, our Creator

3. Jehovah El Elyon   Genesis 14:22   The Lord, the Most High God, the Owner

4. Jehovah Adonai   Genesis 15:2   The Lord, the Master

5. Jehovah El Olam   Genesis 21:33   The Lord, the Everlasting

6. Jehovah Jireh   Genesis 22:14   The Lord, the Provider

7. Jehovah Rapha   Exodus 15.26   The Lord, the Healer

8. Jehovah Nissi   Exodus 17:15   The Lord, the Banner

9. Jehovah Makaddesh   Exodus 31:13   The Lord, our Sanctifier

10. Jehovah Shalom   Judges 6:24   The Lord, our Peace

11. Jehovah Shaphat   Judges 11:27   The Lord, the Judge

12. Jehovah Saboath   I Samuel 1:3   The Lord of Hosts

13. Jehovah Tsidkenu   Jeremiah 23:6   The Lord, our Righteousness

14. Jehovah Raah   Psalms 23:1   The Lord, the Shepherd

15. Jehovah Elyon   Psalms 7:17   The Lord, the Blesser

16. Jehovah Hosenu   Psalms 95:6   The Lord, the Maker

17. Jehovah Gibbor   Isaiah 42:13   The Lord, the Mighty

18. Jah-Jehovah   Isaiah 12:2, 26:4 The Lord, the Jehovah

19. Jehovah Shammah   Ezekiel 48:35   The Lord, the Ever Present

20. Jehovah Jehoshua   Matthew 1:21,   The Lord Jesus Christ
    Messiah   Acts 2:36

PERSONAL STUDY NOTES

1. READING: Mark 16:17

   COMMENT: Signs are not important for what they do, but are finger posts pointing to higher power.

2. READING: 1 John 3:23

   COMMENT: We are commanded to have faith in His name.

3. READING: Exodus 20:7

   COMMENT: The word "take" means "to wear". Vain means without signs, anything which disappoints hope.

4. READING: Jude 1 - 25 (*verse 12)

   COMMENT: Clouds with no water are unable to produce.

5. READING: Mark 7:13

   COMMENT: Religiosity, false prophets to the utmost

6. READING: Acts 4:12

   COMMENT: Saving name

7. READING: Acts 2:21

   COMMENT: Lives get changed in this place by Jesus' name , not Buddah, Mohammed, Krishna, or Joseph Smith.

8. READING: Acts 1:3

   COMMENT: God wants us to be infallible proofs.

9. READING: Acts 1:8

   COMMENT: Refer to John 14, Luke 22, 1 John 3.

10. READING: Proverbs 14:25

   COMMENT: A true witness (one who tells truth/word) delivereth souls.

11. READING: Acts 4:13 - 33

COMMENT: We witness with the Name of Jesus.

12. READING: Acts 3:1 - 21

COMMENT: Jesus' Name is the healing Name!!! There are infallible proofs!

13. READING: Acts 16:18

COMMENT: Delivering name

14. READING: John 16:23

COMMENT: Jesus' Name is your rod of authority.

15. READING: Exodus 14:1 - 16

COMMENT: Stretch forth the rod/name.

16. READING: John 17:6

COMMENT: Jesus did, and we must, manifest that family name! (ie. - family dower rights, power of attorney, ambassadors; blank check signed by Jesus)

. . . .

RENAMED AND REDEEMED
TEST

THIS IS AN OPEN BOOK TEST.
ON MULTIPLE CHOICE QUESTIONS, SELECT THE BEST ANSWER.

1. **When Adam chose to eat of the tree of the knowledge of good**
    and evil, he got just what he asked for:

    a. He knew Eve, his wife, and she bare him a son.
    b. The knowledge of every evil disease and atrocity.
    c. The awareness of every good and perfect gift that lay just beyond his sin-infected reach.
    d. Both B and C.

2. **The awfulness of sin is:**

    a. I inherited sin and death.
    b. My bloodline is contaminated.
    c. The Adamic nature is present at birth, and it works its deadly work.
    d. All of the above.

3. **Paul, in Romans 7:24, expresses the heart cry of all**
    humanity. He stated:

    a. The soul that sinneth, it shall die.
    b. For God so loved the world that he gave his only begotten Son.
    c. Jesus wept.
    d. Oh, unhappy and pitiable and wretched man that I am, who will release and deliver me from (the shackles of) this body of death?

4. **Sin can be covered by:**

    a. Confession to one another.
    b. Hell.
    c. Doing it in secret.
    d. The blood of Jesus.
    e. Both B and D.

5. **The ground is cursed, and man must toil to eat of it because:**

    a. There has been a drought.
    b. Of the original sin in the Garden of Eden.
    c. He has the wrong tools.
    d. None of the above.

6. **Satan's opposition had no effect on Jesus. It should have no effect on me.**

    a. True.
    b. False.

7. **Faith comes to us by:**

    a. Singing songs in church.
    b. Financial contributions to the ministry.
    c. Hearing God's word.
    d. Telling others about Jesus.

8. **Your way out of whatever is troubling you depends on:**

    a. Hearing and obeying God's word.
    b. Meeting with a counselor on a regular basis.
    c. Hearing God's word and then deciding what part of it to follow.
    d. All of the above.

9. **A good way to tell whether God is moving in a church is to find one with:**

    a. A beautiful building.
    b. Happy old people.
    c. A television ministry.
    d. Talented singers.

10. **Prosperity is a family affair. That means:**

    a. Your decisions always affect more than just you.
    b. God will bless you with children.
    c. Families should always go shopping together.
    d. All of the above.

MATCHING: (11-14) SELECT THE BEST ANSWER FROM A THROUGH E.
THERE WILL BE ONE ANSWER LEFT OVER.

11. **Having done all _____.**

12. **God promised to satisfy us with _____.**

13. **For God's laws to work for us, we must_____.**

14. **Turn not from God's law, and you shall_____.**

a. prosper
b. obey
c. stand
d. long life
e. all of the above

15. **The only way to success is to understand that:**

  a. The value of money is declining.
  b. Our source is God.
  c. Our employers are doing the best they can to help us.
  d. It is the small foxes that spoil the vine.

16. **We make full use of His redemption when we take:**

  a. His Name.
  b. His word.
  c. His spirit.
  d. Full advantage of the church's outreaches.

TRUE OR FALSE: (17-21) MARK "A" FOR TRUE OR "B" FOR FALSE.

17. **Romans 8:1 says, ''there is therefore now no conviction to them which are in Christ Jesus, who walk not after the flesh, but after the Spirit.''**

18. **Parents never tire of seeing themselves reproduced in their children. Our heavenly Father is no different. He wants to see His characteristics in us, e.g., love, peace and joy.**

19. **The Holy Ghost introduces us to the Father.**

20. **Sonship means to be an heir to the Heavenly Father.**

21. The mark of true Sonship is the ability to give orders.

22. Romans 5:19 says, "For as by one man's disobedience many were made sinners, so by the obedience of one shall many be made righteous." The men referred to in this scripture are:

a. Noah and Christ.
b. Adam and King David.
c. Peter and Christ.
d. Adam and Christ.

23. **My hope of glory is:**

a. My righteousness.
b. Christ in me.
c. Living a godly life-style.
d. A strong prayer life.
e. Faithful church attendance.

24. **Everything we appropriate from the spirit realm is obtained through:**

a. The agency of faith.
b. Spiritual warfare.
c. Calling the church for prayer.
d. Having hands laid on us.
e. All of the above.

25. **Even when we don't have faith in something, God is still pleased when we hope and pray.**

a. True.
b. False.

26. **God's word says, "whosoever shall _____ shall be saved."**

a. Be anointed with oil by the elders of the church.
b. Be slain in the spirit while dancing at the front of the sanctuary.
c. Call upon the name of the Lord.
d. Leap the highest before the Lord.
e. Both A and D above.

27. **If you are beset by Satan's snares, you will receive deliverance by:**

    a. Anointing your forehead with oil and shouting loudly.
    b. Calling ten people together to form a circle around you as you lay prostrate on the floor.
    c. Calling on the Lord.
    d. Calling your Pastor immediately, especially if it is after midnight.

28. **Since God is so far away from us, we can't expect our prayer to reach Him in less than 24 hours.**

    a. True.
    b. False.

29. **Even though Jesus is not sick, the world that we live in is cursed; therefore, we cannot expect to walk free from sickness until we get to heaven.**

    a. True.
    b. False.

30. **Jesus defeated Satan as:**

    a. The son of man.
    b. The Son of God.

31. **The more the children of Israel were afflicted by their captors, the more they multiplied and grew.**

    a. True.
    b. False.

32. **God said that He would give us the heathen for our inheritance.**

    a. True.
    b. False.

33. **The author and finisher of our faith is:**

    a. God.
    b. Jesus.
    c. The Holy Spirit.
    d. All of the above.

34. Titus 3:7 says, "being justified by His _____, we should be made heirs according to the hope of eternal life."

    a. Blood.
    b. Faith.
    c. Mercy.
    d. Grace.
    e. A and C above.

35. Jesus died for us so we could go to heaven, but it is up to us to defend ourselves here on earth.

    a. True.
    b. False.

36. The way we feel about ourselves determines whether or not we are counted righteous.

    a. True.
    b. False.

37. The Holy Spirit has been sent as our covenant attorney to ensure our inheritance.

    a. True.
    b. False.

38. God judges the world:

    a. Based on His mercy.
    b. According to His understanding of our weaknesses.
    c. Based on love.
    d. In righteousness.
    e. By fire.

TRUE OR FALSE: (39-43) SELECT "A" FOR TRUE OR "B" FOR FALSE.

39. The Bible says: "For the eyes of the Lord are upon the righteous, and his ears are open unto their cry. The face of the Lord is against them that do evil."

40. God's grace is frustrated by our carnal efforts.

41. God's grace is a gift, but the amount of grace extended toward us is determined by our efforts.

42. When Jesus died for us, the biggest part of our debt was atoned for. The rest of our debt is erased by our faithfulness.

43. When you are living in sin, the Lord will not hear you when you call unto Him.

44. God's greatest blessing to us is:

   a. Having beautiful churches to worship in.
   b. Being able to claim a tax exemption on money given to the church.
   c. Deliverance.
   d. All of the above.

45. Praise brings:

   a. Results.
   b. Peace.
   c. Happiness.
   d. Strength.

46. The correct scripture reference for ''Greater is He that is in you than he that is in the world'' is:

   a. Colossians 2:14.
   b. 1 John 5:18.
   c. 1 John 4:4.
   d. None of the above.

47. Scripture teaches us that we can get to a place in God where the wicked one touches us not.

   a. True.
   b. False.

48. Faith is staring at adversity and praising God.

   a. True.
   b. False.

49. **We must fight against the people that represent evil. After all, God placed us here to represent Him.**

   a. True.
   b. False.

50. **Our warfare is:**

   a. How strongly and loudly we pray.
   b. Based on our knowledge of the people we are fighting.
   c. Not necessary.
   d. The fight of faith.

51. **Jesus prayed that God wouldn't take us out of the world, but that He would keep us from evil.**

   a. True.
   b. False.

52. **The Bible says that casting out devils is a sign that shall follow them that believe.**

   a. True.
   b. False.

53. **Satan is never surprised at God's plan of deliverance for His people, since Satan can see in the spirit realm.**

   a. True.
   b. False.

54. **God hardened the heart of Pharaoh. Why?**

   a. Because God felt mean.
   b. God did not harden the heart of Pharaoh.
   c. So that the Egyptians would know that He was the Lord.
   d. A and C above.

55. God's plan of deliverance may include us being in an uncomfortable position.

    a. True.
    b. False.

56. Satan has a plan to take you out. God has a plan to keep you in. This means that God will not take us out of the world, but will keep us from the evil.

    a. True.
    b. False.

57. The word "life" is a good substitute for the word "quicken" in the Bible.

    a. True.
    b. False.

58. God quickens us because:

    a. Of His mercy.
    b. He loves us.
    c. He wants to be served.
    d. None of the above.
    e. Both A and B above.

59. Jesus said, that the words He spoke to us were:

    a. Love and mercy.
    b. Mercy and goodness.
    c. Spirit and life.
    d. Life and love.
    e. All of the above.

TRUE OR FALSE: (60-65) SELECT "A" FOR TRUE OR "B" FOR FALSE

60. It is possible for God to lie.

61. It is impossible to have life without having the Son of God.

62. The very same Spirit that raised Christ Jesus from the dead can also live in me.

63. Sometimes God will make us bait in the rat trap to catch Satan. A good example of this is when Pharaoh pursued Israel to the Red Sea.

64. Genesis 1:27 says, "So God created man in His own image." From this we are to under stand that God is male.

65. Scripture tells us that "as he is, so are we in this world." The reverse of this is also true. Whatever we have done, it is as though He did it and paid the penalty for it.

66. In Acts 3:6, Peter said to the lame man, "Silver and gold have I none; but such as I have give I thee: In the name of Jesus Christ of Nazareth rise up and walk." The lame man was healed. What did Peter have that he gave to the lame man?

    a. The glory of God.
    b. The mercy of God.
    c. The power of God.
    d. All of the above.

67. A person is known by his:

    a. Attitude toward work.
    b. Family.
    c. Wealth.
    d. Name.

68. The Holy Ghost is a gift to man.

    a. True.
    b. False.

69. When you take the name of Jesus, you have:

    a. His position of honor with the Father.
    b. His knowledge.
    c. His substance.
    d. None of the above.

70. **Our power and authority hinges upon:**

   a. Our lot in life.
   b. Our financial status.
   c. Our physical stature.
   d. Our submission to Jesus.
   e. All of the above.

71. **When Philip asked Jesus to show him the Father, Jesus answered him by saying, "he that hath seen me hath seen the Father." This means:**

   a. Jesus looked like His Father.
   b. Jesus was in submission to His Father and was only doing and saying those things that He was instructed.
   c. The Father appeared to Philip, but Philip was sleeping and didn't wake up to see Him.
   d. None of the above.

72. **Failure to submit to Jesus:**

   a. Is a sin.
   b. Is not that big of a deal. Jesus knows we are mere flesh.
   c. Can cause us to lose our chance of going to heaven.
   d. Is expected due to our Adamic nature.
   e. A and C above.

73. **The Bible says if we submit ourselves to God and resist the devil:**

   a. He will flee from us.
   b. He will come against us seven times stronger.
   c. He will ignore us.
   d. None of the above.

74. **It is possible to be a friend of the world and a friend of God.**

   a. True.
   b. False.

75. **If we ask the Father for something in Jesus' name:**

   a. He laughs at us.
   b. He is displeased with us.
   c. He will give it to us.
   d. He expects us to join with an intercessor.

76. Submission to God always wins the victory.

    a. True.
    b. False.

77. When we take His name, we are pledging to do all He did. We assume His posture and attitude toward the lost and dying. Therefore:

    a. We know, as Jesus knew, that the Father is the source.
    b. Through faith in prayer, we defeat Satan.
    c. We will represent Him in prayer.
    d. All of the above.
    e. A and B above.

78. Psalm 54:1 says, "Save me, O God, by thy name, and judge me by thy strength." This means we are saved through His name.

    a. True.
    b. False.

79. Scripture tells us that we shall receive _____ after that the Holy Ghost is come upon us.

    a. God's love.
    b. Power.
    c. Mercy.
    d. All of the above.

80. We represent Him in drawing others to Jesus.

    a. True.
    b. False.

81. God is represented by His people through supernatural works.

    a. True.
    b. False.

82. **Why did Jesus go into the wilderness to be tempted of the devil?**

   a. To prove that He was something.
   b. He didn't go into the wilderness to be tempted of the devil.
   c. He was led there by the Spirit.
   d. None of the above.

83. **We represent Jesus:**

   a. By commanding demons in His Name.
   b. Through supernatural works.
   c. In resisting the devil.
   d. In drawing others to Jesus.
   e. All of the above.

84. **If I pray in my name, I can expect:**

   a. Great and mighty things which I know not.
   b. 1,000 to flee.
   c. 10,000 to flee.
   d. Only what I can do.
   e. A and B above.

85. **Isaiah 55:11 states, "My word...shall not return unto me void", but:**

   a. "It shall be effectual and fervent, powerful and effective."
   b. "It shall accomplish that which I please, and it shall prosper in the thing whereto I sent it."
   c. Both A and B.
   d. None of the above.

86. **Which statement is correct?**

   a. I must pray to the Father, in the Name of Jesus, through the Holy Spirit, according to the word.
   b. I must pray to the Holy Spirit, in the Name of the Father, through the blood of Jesus, according to the word.
   c. I must pray to Jesus, in the Name of the Holy Spirit, by the grace of the Father, according to the word.
   d. I must pray by the leading of the Holy Spirit, by the blood of Jesus, to the Father.
   e. None of the above.

87. **Suffering is always due to sin.**

   a. True.
   b. False.

MATCHING: (88-92) SELECT ONE LETTER ANSWER PER NUMBER.

88. **Shepherd**

89. **Resurrection and Life**

90. **Vine**

91. **Bread**

92. **Door**

   a. Sustainer
   b. Way, Entrance
   c. Life Giver, Death Destroyer
   d. Satisfier, Food
   e. Keeper, Caregiver

93. **Select the corresponding item for YAHWEH.**

   a. The Lord, the Healer.
   b. The Lord, the Shepherd.
   c. I Am that I Am.
   d. The Lord, the Banner.

94. **Select the corresponding item for The Lord, the Provider.**

   a. Jehovah Shalom.
   b. Jehovah Jireh.
   c. Jehovah Rapha.
   d. Jehovah Tsidkenu.

95. **The same Spirit that gave Jesus life gives me life.**

   a. True.
   b. False.

96. **We are commanded to have:**

   a. Faith in His name.
   b. Love for our family.
   c. Hope in the word.
   d. Peace in the world.

97. **The rod of our authority is:**

    a.   Polished oak.
    b.   Jesus' blood.
    c.   God's grace.
    d.   Jesus' name.

98. **Vain means without signs; anything which disappoints hope.**

    a.   True.
    b.   False.

99. **Acts 1:3 tell us that:**

    a.   A true witness delivereth souls.
    b.   We witness with the Name of Jesus.
    c.   God wants us to be infallible proofs.
    d.   None of the above.

100. **Exodus 20:7 says, ''Thou shalt not take the name of the LORD thy God in vain; for the LORD will not hold him guiltless that taketh his name in vain.''**

    a.   True.
    b.   False.

TEST ANSWER KEY

The answers to the test questions have been supplied so that you will be able to grade you own test.
Please do not send your test to us.

1. D	36. B	71. B
2. D	37. A	72. E
3. D	38. D	73. A
4. E	39. A	74. B
5. B	40. A	75. C
6. A	41. B	76. A
7. C	42. B	77. D
8. A	43. B	78. A
9. B	44. C	79. B
10. A	45. D	80. A
11. C	46. C	81. A
12. D	47. A	82. C
13. B	48. A	83. E
14. A	49. B	84. D
15. B	50. D	85. B
16. A	51. A	86. A
17. B	52. A	87. B
18. A	53. B	88. E
19. A	54. C	89. C
20. A	55. A	90. A
21. B	56. A	91. D
22. D	57. A	92. B
23. B	58. E	93. C
24. A	59. C	94. B
25. B	60. B	95. A
26. C	61. A	96. A
27. C	62. A	97. D
28. B	63. A	98. A
29. B	64. B	99. C
30. A	65. A	100. A
31. A	66. C	
32. A	67. D	
33. B	68. A	
34. D	69. C	
35. B	70. D	